Worcester's Guildhau

An Historical Guide

Jeff Carpenter

BREWIN
BOOKS

First published by Brewin Books Ltd

Studley, Warwickshire B80 7LG

in April 2000

ISBN 1 85858 158 3

British Library Cataloguing in Publication Data

A Catalogue record for this book is available from the British Library

Guildhall Front Elevation Photograph

©Oxford Picture Library / Philip Ruler

Typeset in Times and

Made and Printed by

Heron Press, Kings Norton,

Birmingham

Jeff Carpenter

- a former Mayor of Worcester has an abiding interest in both the city and its people. He has also written Wartime Worcestershire (Brewin Books) and is the editor of a series of local historic maps. He dedicates this text to his parents and all those others who have loved Worcester. All profits go to the Mayor's Charity.

Worcester's Guildhall

An Historical Guide

Introduction by Henry Sandon

It is both a joy and honour to be asked to write an introduction to Jeff Carpenter's Historical Guide to Worcester's Guildhall.

This lovely building has played a major part in the life of the City, and while its beauty is evident for all to see, it is the great history, famous visitors and fine treasures which make it really special.

What pleasure it gives to know that you are treading where royalty trod (George the Third, Queen Victoria and our present Queen) or heroes like Lord Nelson and Sir Winston Churchill received the Freedom of the City of Worcester.

As a lover of Worcester porcelain, my favourite pieces in the Guildhall are the superb pair of jugs painted with the Corporation arms and dated 1757 which I was allowed to borrow during the BBC Antiques Roadshow recording in Worcester Cathedral, and the lovely pair of punch bowls painted with portraits of King George the Third and Queen Charlotte by John Pennington in 1792. Do see these especially the portrait of Charlotte who patriotically wears around her head a ribbon inscribed "GOD SAVE THE QUEEN"

The book will help you to uncover the history of this great building that the architect Sir Gilbert Scott described as "the most valued building in your city next to the Cathedral".

Yours sincerely

Henry Sandon.

A Guildhall Grotesque

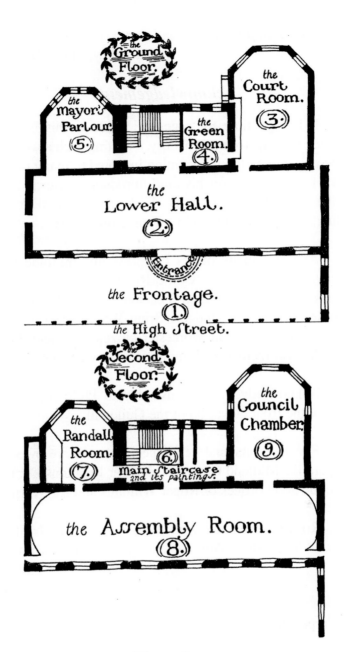

Floor plan
Suggested Tour Plan - Follow the Numbers.

5

"Worcester that poor, proud and pretty city"

Vesta Tilley, Music Hall Artiste.

Acknowledgements

It is high time for a general guide to this building so crammed with Worcester's history. Writing such a work would not be possible, without becoming indebted to many people. I thank Henry Sandon for his kind introduction, Susan Attwood for her splendid illustrations, Barbara Ronchetti for proof reading, and David Attwood for typing up the text.

Amongst many others I express my gratitude to Mike Grundy, Bill Gwilliam, Colin Roberts, Phil Murray, Tim Bridges, Will Scott, Karen Pearson, Penny Macbeth, Jane Thorniley Walker, Jo Hodges, Brian Whitmore, also to many mayors, councillors and Worcester citizens. I also thank the many cheerful members of my local history classes.

Acknowledgement is also due to Philip Ruler for the image of the front elevation of the Guildhall.

For their financial help, special thanks are owed to the Co-operative Midland Counties Member Relations Committee, and to the good offices of Roger Williams and Ray Turner.

Royalties from this work are donated to the charity of the Mayor of Worcester. Any mistakes alas remain my own.

Jeff Carpenter.

Charles 1st

The Old Building

Sadly we have no picture of the old timbered Guildhall with its piazza and adjoining shops. Inside the actual hall there were two busy courts of justice with a prison to the right of the Nisi Prius Court, and almost opposite to it, the jailer's dwelling which was additionally an alehouse for serving prisoners. By 1601 space had been added for storing arms and weapons in case of public disorder. Hectic times had also provided the opportunity to employ recycled building materials. The wood of a carved rood loft from St. Andrews was bought for sixteen shillings and stone was taken from the Old High Cross when it was demolished in 1563.[1]

What a noisy, overburdened building this must have been, for Worcester was no provincial backwater[2] but active in trade communications and in promoting the dramatic new religious changes. As for the Corporation, they seemed keen to exploit every ounce of their power, imposing heavy tolls on vessels using the Severn and even leasing their own coalmines out on the border with Shropshire.[3]

A great deal of the bustle came from the work of the courts; the county petty and quarter sessions, grand juries, assizes (after 1621 both for county and city) special orphans courts, and the occasional but important business connected with the Council of the Marches. In 1546 John Davis, a stalwart Protestant described what it was like to be confined in chains in the freezing Guildhall dungeons.[4] Much later in 1679 the notorious Popish Plot trial of the Jesuit, Father John Wall would have been held here before Judge Atkins - the charge - high treason - the penalty to be hung, drawn and quartered at the top of Red Hill.

There was much coming and going of officials. A town clerk *(hominum probus)* had existed since 1476 and as well as the sheriff, two chamberlains and a water bailiff, there were sundry others: - macebearers, constables, aletasters, searchers of cloth and leather, a piggard and bellman "to walk the night"[5]. In 1639 the Corporation also appointed their own preacher or lecturer.

Entertainment's and 'heavy' junketing were very much the vogue. The *Journal of Prior More* described dining with "ye bailiffs and all skarlet gowns" drinking malmsey, osey, red wine, rumsey, sack, pyment, hoppocras, claret and Rhenish wine (though probably on ecclesiastical premises). By 1585 the Guildhall had its own band of occasional musicians or waites, but the performance of plays was forbidden in 1627 "because of the tippling and drinking —- foreasmuch as we find the glass windows of the council chamber to be much broken"

The damage inflicted in the Civil War was more serious, Worcester tradition claims that it was in this part of the High Street the Royalists made their last stand. The civic sword was dragged off, but fortunately not the precious charters. Bodies of wounded soldiers were brought in from the street so that afterwards the building would require drastic disinfection — "Paid for stonpitch and rosen to perfume the hall after the Scots - 2d."

A city taken by storm could expect no mercy and the Parliamentary army's mood was of vengeful grimness. One of the rare sources of restraint and clemency was Edward Elvins, Cromwell's choice as military govenor. Did the solicitaions in high places of this former mayor and sheriff prevent even greater savagery? -"It may be partly due to Edward Elvins that Worcester Cathedral is still standing" states the historian, Philip Styles* - if that was true he probably saved the old Guildhall as well.

*See Philip Styles. The City of Worcester During the Civil Wars in The English Civil Wars; Local Aspects (Edited by R.C Richardson. Sutton Publishing 1997)

After 1651 the building like the city suffered years of post war neglect though stones were taken from the demolished military walls to "quoin the Town Hall*" It was expected that Charles II would make a triumphant return,dispensing gratitude and largesse to corporation and citizens. He never came, nor did he pay a jot towards any town hall building restoration as happened at Bridgenorth. The only state visit was by James II in the next reign - an unmitagated disaster and a major civic humiliation. Meanwhile the place was structurally unsound and woefully inadaquate - all in all the time for a complete rebuilding was long overdue.

THE NEW GUILDHALL

The New Guildhall

"The most valued building in your city, next to the Cathedral"

The new Guildhall had been up for less than a hundred and fifty years when ominous cracks began to appear. But was it, people asked, so much a disaster as an opportunity? Was this the chance to construct something grand and neo-gothic - as prestigious for Victorian Worcester as Waterhouse's new town hall had been for Manchester? Opinion was divided, but by 1875 there were elaborate plans for pulling down and starting again.

It was not a question of opposition but furious opposition. Sir Gilbert Scott, the most famous architect of the day told the Corporation straight; they were about to earn themselves "a most unenviable notoriety" in destroying "a national example of architecture" - "the most valued building in your city, next to the Cathedral"[6] Happily the message got through and good sense prevailed; there would be no rebuilding, but instead a compromise solution (or was it total capitulation?) with Scott himself brought in to preside over an extensive restoration.

It had been a lucky break. The rescued building would later be described by Pevsner as a town hall as "splendid as any of the 18th century in England"[7]. Its original construction, planned in 1717, had been substantially completed by 1724. Valentine Green, that well known observer of the 18th century Worcester scene, referred to it in his usual extravagant prose as a "new edifice, elegant and superb". Without doubt it was an immediate success - henceforth never to be left out of any illustrated city prospect or plan.

The "new edifice" would be widely used. Prestigious law cases in the city and county assizes called for a grander setting than the old Guildhall. And Worcestershire's polite society had long been clamouring for a genteel venue for its assemblies and soirees. Alas, there was the awkward question of cost; there were few sources of finance - principally subscriptions from county grandees and some degree of subsidy from the Worcester Corporation, as ever strapped for cash. Fortunately the scheme enjoyed the patronage of Lord Somers, a 'local boy made good' and the formidable legal mind behind the 1689 English Constitution - a man with the vision and contacts to get things done.

The Frontage

The design of the new building, in somewhat old fashioned baroque was submitted by an elusive[8] stonemason cum architect, Thomas White, who had worked with Christopher Wren and had already been admitted a freeman of Worcester on the strength of his earlier craftsmanship. The frontage is forcefully splendid, with three central bays bearing above the segmental pediment enclosing White's magnificent Roman trophy. At the entrance, a smaller pediment is used, deliberately broken off in order to display the City's heraldic arms to greater advantage. As for the windows, they have flamboyance all of their own, each capped by a grotesque stone head. (Could features that savage ever have belonged to Worcester, one asks?)

But such a bold and vigorous style was not without a purpose. It has been suggested the architect might have been toying with the design of a small European palazzo.[9] Even more important was the need to compel respect for the majesty of the English Law. This was symbolised by the five dominant sculptured figures - towering skywards on the parapet above - in their different ways five commentaries upon Justice. The main door was also made deliberately wide to enable the two assize judges to enter, side by side in their flowing robes without losing dignity.

Oliver Cromwell As the Devil

The Guildhall's strong pictorial imagery, distinctively royalist in sympathy, invited the belief that sound law derived from firm kingship. The theme was emphasised by the presence of three Stuart monarchs with statues of Charles I, Charles II and Queen Anne prominently displayed round and about the entrance. To reinforce the same message, the demonised head of Cromwell was placed over the doorway - his ears fastly nailed: for these royalist builders were out to make propaganda by spreading the myth that the Parliamentary leader had defeated the Crown in 1651 only after selling his soul to the Devil in Nunnery Wood.[10]

Looking up to the bellicose trophy we see that royalty, war and loyalty are still the central, themes. Supported by angels, the imperial arms of England and Hanover are triumphantly displayed as an affirmation of English royal continuity. "Its down with the Jacobites - Long live George I"

The Forecourt

The cost of the building had included money for two paviers, John Brown and James Hill, though by 1802 their work had been replaced by an elaborate pattern of cobbles in honour of Lord Nelson. These in turn were grubbed up sometime during the 19th century. John Noake, mayor and antiquarian moaned about their removal at the time of the renovations, but some cobbles were probably lifted earlier - probably too dangerous and too handy as missiles when the populace got themselves into a temper.

No doubt the robust cast iron railings were also defensive, but not the handsome rococo gateway of 1750, crafted at the famed Derbyshire smitheries of Thomas Bakewell. By the later 19th century the gates were so ravaged by Worcester's smog, they required complete refurbishment by Letherans of Cheltenham. The gates had been proudly emblazoned with the heraldic arms of Worcester - a three turreted castle and three black pears. In this instance the heraldic device was incorporated on a single shield, though the City of Worcester was permitted the special privilege of displaying arms on two shields.

The Two Wings

Thomas White went to his deathbed still owed £165 on the Guildhall. What seemed more important was making the building pay, and the two wings added in 1725 and 1727 were clearly viewed as means of raising more revenue. Both wings contained shops at one time or another, but the south wing was originally intended for Judges' lodgings, and the north for a coffee house. The coffee house later became an eating house - the very one used by Sir Charles Hastings to celebrate the first meeting of the body later known as the British Medical Association.

The Cellars

A labyrinth of cavities under the Guildhall probably harked back to the old structure - much lower in the ground. These depths helped to solve the lack of storage space - particularly of the wine cellarage which was needed to cope with the heavy drinking habits of Worcester's 'capital citizens'. There came a time when the old drinking debts had to be paid and one of the earliest actions of the 1835 council was to auction off the wines and vintage ports in the cellars to help finance what was owing.[11]

THE LOWER HALL

The Lower Hall

The new Guildhall must have been crowded and bustling like its predecessor. Space was needed for courts, for cells, and for assembly rooms, as well as for more pedestrian municipal activities. The Lower Hall was always an essential working area, unshowy and possibly a trifle plain compared with Thomas White's glorious exterior. Here on a south wall they hung the antique fire buckets, awaiting the tolling of St. Andrew's church bell - the city's fire alarm. The buckets were paid for by newly elected members of the Corporation, but apparently with no arrangements made to provide any fire fighters. In 1769 they put out a big fire in Mealcheapen Street only after plying a group of soldiers with plentiful supplies of drink.

The two courtrooms were in constant use, both originally opening straight onto the hall. The *Nisi Prius*, or civil court was on the site of the mayor's parlour, with the criminal court housed in the larger room further along, and still known as the Court Room. Such was the sheer noise of proceedings that blocking off the alcoves became an absolute necessity. Without some element of privacy we can only imagine the harshness of those judicial occasions described by John Noake as the "grim accompaniments of an assize court" -"the arbitrament of life or death upon wretched criminals"[12]

The Lower Hall balconies have always come into their own at election time for speakers to address or harangue the crowd below, though that at the south end was once located in a court room. Elections were always lively in Worcester, and particularly boisterous in the 18th century when the voting was restricted to freemen - a system wide open to irregularity and corruption.

Freemen and Honorary Freemen

Inscribed in gold leaf on a board of honour are the names of past honorary freemen. Worcester conferred this special privilege sparingly upon individuals deemed 'influential' or 'useful', or upon those contributing outstanding service. Two conspicuous 'freedoms' were the honouring of Sir Edward Elgar in 1905, and Sir Winston Churchill in 1951 when the formal ceremonial was mingled with a degree of junketing. In the earlier centuries the junketing had been more excessive and never more than the 'freedom' banquet of all time which took place in 1687 in the old Guildhall. A nervous Corporation in a dark period of Worcester's history had concluded the best way out of their many troubles was by wining and dining the Lord Lieutenant on an incredibly lavish scale. They even decided *pro tempore* to hand back Worcester's royal charter rather than having it taken away by force.[13]

Before the reforms of the 1830s, voting was for Worcester's freemen only - a restricted but sizeable group amounting to over two thousand by the mid 18th century. As well as Parliamentary elections, they voted for coroners and for the city government or 'Common Council' made up of two bodies, the 24, or senior body 'of the better or more worthy citizens', and the 48, 'of the more worthy or discreet of the citizens'. Freeman enjoyed many trading perks on the side, and bribery, if nor lavish, was well organised. In the words of a 1774 election pamphlet "a freeman has now become in his own opinion as great as an Emperor."

It was without doubt a corrupt system, replete with vested interests, but in practice still possible to dismiss a Corporation member for evil council - *'pro male gubernacione'*, and by the 17th century a councillor could also be struck off for uttering 'approprobrious words', and in one case - that of the unfortunate Richard Beddoes for 'declining into dotage'.[14]

The Lower Hall Collections

The Lower Hall Collections

We see that here Worcester has commemorated many of its significant sons but none of its daughters. And are there not some glaring omissions? There is no portrait of that great 'medic' Sir Charles Hastings, and not a mention of the founders of that culinary relish enjoyed throughout the world - Worcestershire Sauce.

Sir Edward Elgar

Elgar shares a special distinction of being commemorated twice - a portrait by Philip Burne-Jones, and a bust by Donald Gilbert reverentially placed next to the picture of the Queen. Elgar had been strongly influenced by his native city - the Severn and the Worcestershire countryside so often shining through his music. Honours meant so much to him, and he did not conceal his delight at receiving the Freedom of Worcester on 12 September 1905. What was more, the Mayor for that year was his closest boyhood friend, Hubert Leicester. Fame, fortune and creative restlessness took Elgar far from Worcester, but he returned at the end of his life, relishing such local delights as 'the Three Choirs', and the races.

A Gallery of Victorian Enterprise in the Lower Hall

A number of the portraits form a veritable gallery of Victorian enterprise. Of the Worcester industries, gloving is represented by John Dent (1777-1855) and William Dent (1784-1854), leading English glove makers at a time when the wearing of gloves was socially de rigeur. The prosperous Shropshire ironfounding tradition expanded into the city through the nonconformist Richard Padmore, who was also a bank director, and a notable philanthropist. One of the portraits is of Alderman T. Rowley Hill, a committed free churchman and owner of the biggest vinegar works in the world in Lowesmoor, which had additional capacity for producing a range of British fruit wines.

21

Worcester missed out on the early railways, but later began to boom as an industrial railway centre with railway tycoons as influential councillors. One of them was Alexander Clunes Sherriff (1816-1875), founder of the West Midland Railway and proprietor of the Worcester Engine Works, which in its prime employed a thousand 'hands'. Sherriff presented the City with its monumental mayor's chain - whose heavy gold links bore an uncanny resemblance to railway couplings. Walter Holland's concerns were in the fascinating business of railway safety. His firm, McKenzie and Holland made not only oil lamps, but signal systems destined for the far reaches of the Empire.

Sir Arthur Carlton was Worcester's theatrical and cinema impresario. His refurbished Theatre Royal staged everything from pantomime extravaganzas, to the Shakespearean productions of F. R. Benson. In the Great War, Carlton took up the cause of Worcester's servicemen, working tirelessly both to help them and provide suitable memorials to their heroism. (Including the oaken screens in this hall which open to reveal their names cherished for posterity)

Henry Hebb's portrait by Sebastian Cole reminds us of the importance of medical men in Worcester's history. Hebb was an eminent heart specialist who translated an important French medical text into English. As a reforming mayor, he applied his mind to sorting out the terrible muddle into which the city's charitable trusts had fallen. In old age, he was to found local charity almshouses in Worcester for "decayed aldermen and councillors and the widows of such"

Henry Clifton was a stalwart of the old system when Worcester was run by the councils of the 24 and 48, aided by un-elected improvers. As the mayor in November 1831, at the height of the reform agitations, he was hit by a brick whilst reading the Riot Act on the Guildhall steps.

William Lygon, 7th Earl Beauchamp ended his life in exile, driven abroad by the contemporary horror of homosexuality. His early career had shown greatest promise, he was mayor at the age of 24 entertaining some 14,000 citizens at his monster garden parties. The Earl did not need to be a member of the council. In 1896 his aristocratic status was sufficient for him to be awarded the honour of mayor - just as genteel members of the original Worcestershire County Council were invited to sit on a higher dais! Earl Beauchamp's mayoress was his sister, Lady Mary Lygon, who probably inspired one of the Enigma Variations.

Richard Woolf, the splendidly bewhiskered town clerk of 1865, harboured a fierce pride in Worcester's history, encouraging the Corporation to collect and cherish its historic treasures. He did much to stimulate the spirit of traditionalism in the city, but his reputation as an antiquarian was eclipsed by Alderman John Noake - a truly outstanding practitioner of the art.

Mayor Clifton, Enemy of Popular Reform

Justice is Blind

The Other Collections of the Lower Hall

As in other 18th century town halls, it was the custom to keep a small collection of curiosities for the delectation of genteel visitors. An item always likely to inspire interest was the brank, the ancient instrument for punishing scolding women. There was also the brass cannon captured in turn from Arab pirates and a French warship, and presented to the mayor by a passing visitor.

The Court Room when it was in use

The Court Room

Victorians would have known the room well, for here was the setting of the assize court in *East Lynne* - Mrs Henry Wood's most famous novel. Today the courtroom galleries are covered in, the well padded chair of a Corporation dignitary now occupying the space once used by the judge. Cast your eyes up and you see the sculptured head - representing Justice Blindfolded and written beneath some stern advice for those who once administered the court's proceedings - *"Fiat Justitia, Ruat Coelum"* - Let justice be done though the sky falls.

It is now difficult to envisage that there was a way up into the gallery. Behind the gallery was the retiring room, now the Members Room, where juries and grand juries came to their decisions.

In the Court Room on a single Monday in March 1786, seventeen prisoners received the death sentence. The Worcester court attracted eminent attorneys of the calibre of Sir William Jones, 'Orient Jones'.[15] the Sanskritist, poet and future judge of the Indian High Court. Jones in one of his letters mentions a harrowing episode from one Assize session where a young girl - completely deranged in mind was hanged for strangling her bastard child - the law had no power of mitigation.

One of the later trials was the famous 'Garibaldi' case of December 1925, when Herbert Burrows, a local P.C. was charged with a gruesome triple murder at the Garibaldi Inn in Wyld's Lane. The legal proceedings aroused morbid fascination in Worcester after the accused had crassly incriminated himself by disclosing details of the murder to a police colleague before anything was discovered. He then proceeded to plead not guilty in the courtroom.[16]

Civic Pride

When the court function ceased, this was the room given over to the city council's heaviest committee work. Over the years many important policies have been hammered out within these walls - pedestrianisation, bus passes for the elderly, leisure centres, smoke free zones, and much else besides. It may not do much for the cynics, but for those with civic pride in Worcester, this ranks as a very special part of the building.

The Civic Displays in the Court Room

Looking down from the north wall we see the large portrait of William Laslett, in turn both a Liberal and Conservative M.P. and the donor of Worcester's first proper cemetery at Astwood - in its time also regarded as a place for recreational walks. In the later 19th century workers in the city were to form a Trades Council for consolidating activity within the growing labour movement. Their presidential board of honour, here displayed, demonstrated the special contribution of railway and engineering workers and Worcester's 'Co-operators' - many winning a place on the council.

There is also a civic list containing the names of former chamberlains - the honorary officials who were once the treasurers of the city with additional responsibilities like ensuring that swans still remained on the Severn. Another list shows those who were the past sheriffs - powerful officers whose authority stretched back into history. Their duties involved protecting the royal judges, and making sure the walls of Worcester Castle did not fall down - a task incidentally in which they were conspicuously unsuccessful.

The Green Room

In a building used so intensively, it was essential to keep some all purpose space. Primarily this was a counsel chamber for lawyers from the criminal court next door, but it was borrowed from time to time by the card players frequenting the 18th century Assembly Room upstairs - quite a fascinating mixture of uses. In later years the Green Room became the place for more intimate meetings, and for visitors waiting to see the mayor.

The confined dimensions made it specially appropriate for displaying the old picturesque Worcester views we love so well - the images of ancient streets and courts removed in former draconian slum clearance schemes. The room also contains some of the well known prospects of the 18th century city - including S. and N. Buck's engraving of 1732, which shows both the old and new bridges together with a fine flotilla of trading craft moored upon the Severn. There is also an engraving of the original Porcelain Manufactory incorporating the old Warmstry House - extended in 1751 along the riverbank, the kilns occupying the former terraced gardens of the house.

THE MAYOR'S PARLOUR

The Parlour (viewed only by permission)

Today the room radiates all the comfortable imagery of a mayor's parlour with its dark panelling and thick carpets. It was not always so, for at one time it was entirely given over to legal matters. The Victorian police court held there was characterised by its stern attitudes towards the poor of the crowded city centre. Meeting in August 1858, the court sentenced two young Dolday prostitutes "for their brazen insensibility to shame" (Worcester Herald) and in 1898 the magistrates took a hard line with poor German and Italian street musicians, described as "foreigners come for English bounty".[17] In the 18th century the room had housed the prestigious Nisi Prius or Civil Assize, possessing its own gallery with a special inscription over the judges chair :-

"Accessit Magistratibus Auctoritas"
(Authority has been granted to the magistrates)
"Honoratur Recta, Pravca Puniuntur"
((so that) Right should be honoured and wrong-doing punished.)

These words according to Valentine Green derived from the famed Greek classical site at Zant - having been noted and brought to Worcester by George Sandys, the poet and scholarly traveller probably related to Martin Sandys (1672-1753), an influential Town Clerk of the 1730s.

This was the room where on 27th March 1757, heavy chimney stacks from above crashed down onto many of those assembled. Justice Wilmott escaped unscathed, but six were killed and five attorneys injured.

These days weighty issues of law have been banished, and it is the mayors who rule here now, with their mayoral effects, and appendages happily scattered all around. Mayors in Worcester go back to the charter of 1621, the citizens having chafed for centuries under the indignity of possessing only bailiffs as their chief citizens - a higher bailiff and a lower. The change in authority did not necessarily make life easier. Mayor Edward Soley was forced to beg on his knees for the security of the City in September in 1642. Later Mayor Shewringe was sacked for being insufficiently pliable to the Crown, and at least two 18th century mayors, William Winsmore and John Garway ended up as bankrupts.

There were also those illustrious citizens who never made it. Sir Charles Hastings refused because his outstanding medical work did not permit the time. Sir Edward Elgar, it seems, was unofficially invited to become Mayor of Hereford, and it is more than likely he would have been offered Worcester too.[18]

On the eastern wall is the board with gold lettering, listing all mayors since the Municipal Reform Act of 1835. Below it hangs a simple name plaque bearing the name of the current occupant. According to tradition these plaques become the property of the ex-mayors, and should finally be placed on their coffins.

Cap of Liberty in the Assembly Room Plasterwork

The Worcester Corporation Jug, 1757

Some Guildhall Treasures

As well as its more random collections, the Guildhall is home to certain treasured items of considerable historic significance.

The Charters

Royal sheriffs stopped using Worcester Castle as a residence in the 13th century, lessening rigid military control and encouraging the citizens themselves to campaign for greater charter rights through their Corporation and Guilds. These charters - the city's most cherished documents - symbolise the struggle for civic self government from the age of King Alfred. The most empowering of the charters were those of 1189 (Richard I), 1554 (Queen Mary), and especially that of 1621 (James I) when Worcester became a County in its own right. Government may have removed that privilege in 1974, but it remains the ambition of all true patriots to see it restored.

The Sword of State and Maces

The 1621 charter permitted a sword bearer to process before the mayor. (Hereford boasts two!) The official sword presented in 1655 was of fine craftsmanship, bearing the name and mark of the armourer, Peter English. After 1689, the civic authorities to show they were on the winning side, judiciously decided to incise the sword with the arms of William III - adding the name of the mayor, Samuel Taylor, well known for his loyalty to the new constitutional monarchy.

The city's maces have been borne before the bailiffs since at least 1461. The old ones having disappeared in yet another cash crisis, it was decided in 1760 to procure this fine new set still seen well to the fore on all ceremonial occasions.

The Porcelain

Porcelain manufacture and the Guildhall have always been closely linked. It has been argued that there were political considerations behind the decision to establish a porcelain manufactory in the heart of the city.[19] The principal founding partner, Dr John Wall was a Whig activist deeply involved in the goings on at the Guildhall where his father had once been the mayor. It was therefore understandable the Corporation should become an important customer, commissioning two prestigious ring necked jugs from the new manufactory. They now have pride of place on the mayor's sideboard, styled in the fashionable cabbage leaf pattern with scroll handles and bearing the city's arms, boldly painted in onglaze enamels. Made in 1757, the second year of a great imperial sea war - not surprisingly one jug contains the defiant portrait of Britannia ruling the waves.

There is a delightful piece of missing porcelain which properly should grace this room. In 1865 it was decided without a whiff of ratepayers protest that the Corporation of Worcester should purchase the most lavish of wedding presents for the Earl and Countess of Dudley. It would be a service richly gilded and encrusted with pearls, the Raphael like panels painted by Thomas Callowhill. These days the piece is a prize exhibit at the Royal Worcester Porcelain Museum.

The Silver Tank

"The Worcester's have saved the Empire" commented the British Foreign Secretary after the Battle of Gheluvelt. The singular bravery of the second battalion occurred at the crucial stage just as the enemy threatened to break through and cut off Allied communications and the line of retreat. In December 1917 came the recognition. Colonel Hankey, one of the heroes of the hour, representing the Regiment, was awarded the honorary freedom of the city. The scroll of honour was placed in the silver model of a military tank, for Hankey had just been promoted Brigade general of the all important new tank regiment.

(The Lower Hall's elaborate oaken cupboards containing the long list of Worcester men serving in the Great War, can readily be opened for inspection)

THE MAIN STAIRCASE AND ITS PAINTINGS

The Corporation Swordsbearer, Robert Howarth

The Main Staircase and its Significant Portraits

Was there once an elegant staircase here like that of the Old Palace, with long twisted balusters and richly carved tread ends? The Guildhall's 19th century replacement has left us with carved treads and balusters, but of a more robust and serviceable character. To avoid the long climb upstairs there are now urgent plans for a lift.

The staircase boasts its own fine show of municipal portraits:-

William Lewis.

The portrait of the early Victorian mayor, William Lewis by Solomon Cole of Broad Street hangs on the first turning. Lewis was mayor from 1843 to 1846 as the city was attempting to stagger out of serious economic slump. He had started out in tailoring (with a lucrative sinecure as the official distributor of stamps); then launched into banking at a time when its vigorous development was crucial. Lewis was also a force in creating the local Chamber of Commerce and was deeply involved in the early unsuccessful bid to get Worcester onto the national railway network.

On the second turning:-

Robert Howarth: the City Swordbearer, by J Wright.

Who in town was more important than Robert Howarth? Portrayed here in all his finery, bearing the state sword and carrying a pair of Worcester gloves. The swordbearer was a leading influence amongst 'the freemen', the privileged caucus controlling the city's trade and governance. He was entitled to payment from each newly appointed freeman, and also profited from allocating the stallholders in the lucrative fishmarket. In order to qualify for the post, Howarth had first been obliged to resign from the 'Council of the 48', paying the previous holder "ten shillings every Friday night for life". His death, reputedly was from an apoplexy.

The Mayor's Officer.

Frank Barnes is seen in Waldron West's portrait of 1968, dressed in the traditional livery of the Corporation. The haughty pose was readily acceptable from someone was mayor's officer, a proud post traceable back to the Middle Ages, when the first citizens were its bailiffs. One of the principal duties was leading and organising the civic processions. Before 1833, it seems the Mayor's Officer was virtually the city's chief constable.

Joseph Wood. painted by J Rushton. (a well known porcelain artist)

Joseph Wood, mayor in 1860 appeared content to be dressed not in civic flummery, but in the office garb of Worcester's most successful builder. His firm having started in a small way, was responsible for constructing the Shire Hall, City and Count Bank, the Corn Exchange and the Chateau Impney. Joseph Wood's hard work on the bench of magistrates is supposed to have saved the salary of a stipendary. A proud even fierce nonconformist, he became exceedingly unpopular by insisting as mayor on the strictest observation of the 'Lord's day', and forcibly closing shops and pubs during certain hours.

George Williamson

By the 1880s Williamson's had become the city's foremost industrial dynasty, almost monopolising the new market in food and tobacco tins. Having fought in the American Civil War, the younger George Williamson threw himself vigorously into the local political scene. As councillor and mayor, he launched an ambitious programme of municipal improvements from electric trams to horse troughs. Since the local press was largely owned by political colleagues, his effort gained wide publicity, including the fierce lobbying to retain Worcester as a county borough. In 1906 he decided to make the bid for Parliament in an election which earned national notoriety for its blatant corruption. An official inquiry held at the Guildhall brought out the scale of the bribery involved. In the words of one St. John's Ward voter - "I always had half a crown a' parliamentary and I shall not go without it".[20] As a result of the enquiry, the Worcester Constituency was disfranchised for two years.

Samuel Southall by Walter Urwick.

Town Clerk for fifty years, Samuel Southall was appropriately painted in his legal attire. In the past, the office had attracted lawyers of the calibre of Sir Thomas Street, who became a judge ready to defy the king himself. When Worcester became a county borough under late Victorian local government changes, Samuel Southall's legal and administrative skills became especially valuable. So much so he was rewarded with the position of mayor.

Rosina Palmer M.B.E. (painted by E Waldron West).

The Palmers, Rosina and Thomas, were very much a new breed on the council - Labour and 'Co-op'. In 1890 an exhibition of Co-op made goods had been rudely refused entry to the Guildhall - it was argued "they would injure the building". Rosina Palmer's mayoralty helped to change all that. Affordable housing, clearing slums, and social schemes now found their way into the council's policies.[21]

Diana Ogilvy M.B.E.

Somerville painted her graciously à la mode as Worcester's first woman mayor. Miss Ogilvy had earned distinction running a busy Red Cross Hospital at Battenhall in the Great War but her true moment of glory was the official visit by Edward, Prince of Wales in 1932, an occasion marked by great pomp and fierce protestations of loyalty, although Worcester was in the depths of economic depression.

W. B. Williamson.

The Mayor in 1883, W. B. Williamson was, despite his yeomanry uniform, very much the prominent industrialist. After moving from Wolverhampton with a few key workers, he built up a successful trade in tinplate goods at the Providence Works (and was the father of George Williamson). A member of the Plymouth Brethren and a strict abstainer, he also helped to strengthen Masonic influence in the city.

The Randall Room

In 1835 the first elected council stopped meeting in the Assembly Room, and for many years this became the Council Chamber. Today it is a 'memento room' housing all manner of gifts, paintings, prints and trophies presented to the city. Occupying pride of place are the three wall plaques commemorating Worcester's war effort on the Home Front. At that time the building was a hectic organising centre with victory fairs, savings campaigns, food exhibitions and much besides. Some Guildhall rooms were out of use because they were needed to store aluminium scrap.

Shrewdly surveying the scene is a photographic portrait of George Randall the famously pragmatic council leader of the 1980s. 'George' as he was widely known, presided over a period of uplift and improvements after the doldrum years when council policy was described in the national press as "a race to see who could ruin the town first".

THE ASSEMBLY ROOM

The Assembly Room

"One of the most splendid public rooms to be found in England", claimed Valentine Green - "furnished throughout in a style of dignified taste". Its principal function was meant to be the Council Chamber for the Corporation of Worcester,[22] but in practice it was the smartest meeting place in town - a "magnificent apartment" for the concourse of polite society. In 1791 the room became even more splendid when the London architect, George Byfield, created extensions at both ends, inserting shallow apses screened with columns - in the opinion of Valentine Green "so judicious and complete". Each apse was tastefully decorated with plasterwork incorporating two versions of the arms of Worcester, set off at one end by the cap of maintenance, and at the other end, the Phrygian cap of liberty.

So under twelve elegant chandeliers, the genteel would have gathered for assemblies, soirées and diversions of all sorts, but above all for music and dancing, afterwards dispersing into adjacent spaces for coffee and cardplaying. In 1765 Jonathan Swift was here, idling his time away and slandering "the inhabitants" in a good deal of malicious chatter. In 1788 there was a much heralded visit by King George III who pronounced the Assembly Room "a handsome gallery" and proposed a toast, "Prosperity to the City and Corporation of Worcester".

During the 19th century, the room was constantly in use, often for grand occasions like the visit in 1825 of Charles Mathews and his comic theatre (hugely esteemed by Charles Dickens) who staged three performances involving quantities of extravagant props and bulky scenery.

In 1866 the long process of restoration began - a twelve year saga almost as agonising as that of Worcester Cathedral. It began with concern over structural cracks and reached its crescendo in the exotic embellishment of this Assembly Room with its new Italianate ceiling, divided into richly painted and gilded panels to replace Byfield's elegant but simple plasterwork. As an appropriate flourish to complete the refurbishment, Henry Rowe designed a set of customised reproduction furniture with special municipal radiators and fireplaces - the surrounds of the fireplaces being carved by William Forsyth, a member of the celebrated firm of Worcester sculptors.

Assembly Room Collections.

Like the Lower Hall, this was an ideal place to display objects for visitors to view. The choice for this room included Royal Worcester bowls and certain items of Nelson memorabilia to commemorate his wildly popular visit in 1802. There was also a red plush chair reputedly once used by Queen Victoria.

The Assembly Room Paintings.

This was a gallery collected together by admirers of the old order, who were fascinated by the city's royalist connections. Queen Mary was included as the monarch who granted one of Worcester's most significant charters in 1555, Queen Anne because she was the last of the Stuarts and King George III and Queen Charlotte on account of their celebrated visit of 1788 which reached its apogee in this very room. As for the young Queen Victoria, her portrait reminded visitors that she had once resided with her mother, Queen Adelaide, nearby at Great Witley.

The position of Recorder was created in 1621 for high level legal advice and effective lobbying in London. It became the source of great influence. The sixth Earl of Coventry for instance, heir to vast estates at Croome, held such sway, that he as Recorder, rather than the mayor, presented the freedom of Worcester to Nelson. Understandably his portrait by Nathaniel Dance Holland was prominently displayed along with those of other recorders; Sir John Packington, the Earl of Plymouth, and Sir Thomas Winnington, a leading Whig minister under

Walpole. Worcester's greatest legalist Lord Somers does not appear, though his portrait was prominently displayed over the main entrance until it was ruined by "an unskilful restorer" in 1790.

Other Portraits

The 6th Earl Beauchamp was a direct descendent of puissant ancestors, the medieval sheriffs of Worcestershire. In his own right he was a powerful national figure who used his influence to bring Florence Nightingale's new ideas on nursing into Worcester Royal Infirmary.

Mrs Henry Wood's popular and melodramatic novels, thirty nine in total, dealt with a whole range of social issues; drunkenness, strikes, epidemic disease and others - often in a Worcestershire setting. Her books sold in their hundreds of thousands, appearing in many languages including Hindi. Her earlier rival as a Worcester authoress, Mrs Sherwood, was also a moralist but more directly so aiming to imbue the very young with an understanding of hell fire.

Geoffrey Studdert Kennedy, was the devoted priest of the Worcester slums who lived to become the legendary war padre on the Western Front. 'Woodbine Willie', as he became known, was famed for his compassion, for handing out cigarettes at the line. and talking to 'Tommy' in language he could understand. Not least were his skills as a poet able to express the pity and terror of war.

"I will love the things for which they died and I will hate with a bitter lasting hatred the things that brought them to their death."

Richard Fairbairn, here portrayed by Waldron West as the elder statesman in mayoral pose, was probably best remembered as a champion of the underdog :- "Vote, vote, vote for Dickie Fairbairn," as his supporters used to shout. He had come from London to manage the new electrical tramway system, starting his long council career in 1899. Briefly he held the Parliamentary seat for the Liberals after the Great War by exploiting the wider vote. A canny political organiser, his enemies accused him of "egotistical self advertisement and cheapjack appeal to unsophisticated electors." In fact, his success came from campaigning on powerful issues: unemployment, bad housing, and the understanding that many could not afford hospital treatment at Worcester Royal Infirmary.

The Present Council Chamber

Once this was overflow space for social gatherings in the Assembly Room. In the Victorian transformation, the plan was to turn it into an admirable supper room[23] but it became instead, the new council chamber - later embellished with art deco lighting arrangements worthy of the Neasden Odeon.

OUTSIDE THE GUILDHALL

The Guildhall on the Outside

The Rear Yard

The Guildhall was once compared to a gentleman's dress shirt - magnificent at the front - distinctly unprepossessing from the back.   In 1862 the rear of the building became much busier as the City Police Station moved from St. Nicholas Street (despite its "many airy and secure cells") into the Guildhall Yard.   The police were strictly answerable to the Corporation's Watch Committee, who demanded tight constabulary control over the poorer districts, over the doss houses and the drunkenness - Worcester's popular salty mild beer after all had the second highest specific gravity in all England!   The Chief of Police himself lived on site subject to rules, which until the 1920s, forbade him to leave town without the express permission of the mayor, and required him to return his police boots directly to the mayor upon retirement.

Until September 1888 it was the custom to birch very young offenders in the yard, but nearby residents complained of the screaming, so this punishment was transferred out of hearing to the cells beneath the Guildhall Court Room.   This rear yard was also once occupied by Mr Griffiths, the Inspector of Weights and Measures and nearby in 1840 was the space where they parked "Powerful Fire Engine No 3," an appliance maintained by the city's leading insurance companies.[24]   Today the rear area forms that essential appendage to all public buildings - a car park.

Opposite the Guildhall

Almost immediately opposite the Guildhall stood the King's Head, whose "great room" was the home of the 18th century Theatre Royal where Sarah Siddons first trod the boards, (the renown actress having a great love of Worcester 'fat cakes'[25]).   Before that, the room was the location of Worcester's important wool market when it quit the Guildhall. But exactly opposite in 1840 was the city's general market; as readers of Bentley's Directory were duly informed it could be -

"approached from the High Street by a large square entrance, or by one of two smaller arched ones, which form a beautiful stone front, being surmounted by an ornamental and panelled square pediment supported by handsome Tuscan columns."

MEETINGS, MEETINGS
AND
MORE MEETINGS

Meetings, Meetings and More Meetings

The Guildhall was always the special place to congregate. Not that there was a shortage of venues. There were the Assembly Rooms of the *Hop Pole Hotel*, those near the riverside at Diglis and for county occasions after 1834, the Shire Hall. For the city, there was the Public Hall in the Cornmarket, (with seating for 900) after it had closed, as a Music Hall. But the Guildhall always seemed the natural choice for visitations, declarations, elections, exhibitions, fetes, in fact for assemblies of every description.

Some of the endless variety of meetings were to promote good causes like that on 7th. November 1828 to establish the city's first real infants school in Friar Street. Often they were over a single issue, for dare it be said, Worcester enjoys a good argument. In 1764 it was a row about taxation with a lively Guildhall audience loudly insisting on petitioning Parliament against the new charge on cider and perry. Not only did they win, but their success was bucolically celebrated across three counties.

One traditional way of airing your dissatisfaction in Worcester was by getting the mayor to call a 'common hall' or town meeting in the Guildhall. These according to John Noake were well known for "outcries and yellings"[26] and there was no shortage of controversial topics. On 13th April 1809 one was called to demand thorough investigation into the activities of the Duke of York's mistress, Mrs Clarke, accused of securing the purchase of military promotions by using her charms.

Meetings of that kind became increasingly frequent and more outwardly political. 5th November 1831 was one of many assemblies called to debate Parliamentary reform. The platform party supporting reform got loudly cheered whilst their opponents were cried down -"three groans" were given for the Earl of Coventry and three more "for the Corporation". That same night there was rioting outside the building, and the yeomanry were brought in to clear the streets.[27]

During the 1830s and 1840s there were heated debates over many issues:- distress in the glove trade, the ending of slavery, as well as the abolition of the corn laws.   In January 1839, an exchange between Robert Owen, the socialist leader, and John Brindley attracted a vast crowd and ended in utter confusion.   On 23rd February 1842 yet another public meeting was convened to debate the serious state of the economy.   The Guildhall was crammed with the Mayor pleading "for the strictest order and regularity"[28].   Despite this, proceedings were taken over by anti corn law radicals and finally by Chartists, who called for a truly people's parliament by embracing "the principles of the Charter".

One of the most critical economic matters was the need for a modern railway link.   Unfortunately the promotional meetings, well attended and highly enthusiastic were undermined at a crucial stage by a national collapse of financial capital.   The meetings of the Oxford, Worcester and Wolverhampton Railway took place in the Guildhall, and the report to shareholders on 27th August 1847 was made by Isambard Kingdom Brunel himself.

Public health was another big issue and the Guildhall was the setting for the campaign mounted by Sir Charles Hastings in favour of a proper water supply, with proper drainage and sewers.   For all his medical expertise and campaigning spirit, Hastings was condemned by opponents in the Guildhall for extravagance and "unseemly haste".

Our forebears could also become agitated over what we would describe as 'environmental matters'.   In July 1811 it was an argument about destroying "small fish in the Severn".   Later in September 1864 it was a decision over spending a few thousands of council money to prevent the Arboretum and its pleasure gardens being turned into a packed housing estate. Much later in 1894 it would be about purchasing Pitchcroft as open space - but not without opposition from ratepayers.   As one serious objector wrote to the newspaper - "a park of 110 acres is absurd for a city the size of ours - what do THEY want it for?"[29]

Past Elections

Bruising election contests have always ended here, and old style Worcester politics were not more blessed with delicatesse or good manners. Some elections were especially raucous. One of the worst was 1774 when dissenters turning out for the opposition candidate were shouted down as "vipers in your bosom". Even choicer insults were reserved for a bevy of females supporting the official Corporation candidate - "wanton and prating" as they were described - women who had somehow strayed in from "the bagnio" or house of ill repute.[30]

The Future?

Could it be that municipal performance indicators, mission statements or corporate plans will demand an entirely brand new meeting place for the city? It is doubtful if Worcester would ever wear it. Possibly the reverse will happen and the Guildhall as a building of distinction will increasingly come to serve not just the city, but also the nation as a whole. In 1975 E. P. Thompson chose the Assembly Room to deliver an historic indictment of the nuclear arms race[31] - an address banned by the BBC. In 1997 and 1998 the Prime Minister used the Guildhall as a 'media' venue for addressing all the British people. Who knows what next!

The Changing Scene

The Changing Scene
- some reflections on people and policies.

Nobody before or since knew as much about Worcester's history as the Mayor, John Noake. In 1889 he decided to give up the Council - long service and old age had caught up with him - "I now have a bald head, false teeth and an ear trumpet". The young reporter for Berrows Journal had become the seasoned councillor and studious observer of the changing Guildhall in a new era of elected councils. For Noake it was exciting but frightening. "Democracy is now rampant" he complained "May the Lord have mercy on us".[32]

One of Noake's delights was rummaging amongst the documents of St. Swithin's, the most establishment church of the wealthy 18th century Corporation. Its mayoral seat with a flamboyant sword rest was "enriched with frilly swags"[33], and the principal detail of its monument to Mayor Joseph Withers had been carved by John Bacon RA, the sculptor of George III's monument in Westminster Abbey.

Members of this illustrious early Corporation delighted in warming themselves up at various hostelries before putting in an appearance at the Guildhall - the senior body of 'the 24' at *The Globe* in Powick Lane, and 'the 48' at *The Pheasant* in New Street. But did they do all that much when they got to the Guildhall? Worcester's public services as far as they existed seem to have been provided through 'Improvers', legally constituted bodies of well-to-do citizens with parliamentary powers to raise rates for the purpose. In 1823 a special consolidating act was passed "for better supplying the City of Worcester and the Liberties thereof with water and for more effectively paving, lighting, watching and otherwise improving the said city." The Improvers sometimes met in the *Hop Pole* assembly room, but often in the Guildhall. No wonder the other users of the building complained about the cramped conditions. In 1830 the County Grand Jury described the Guildhall as "greatly insufficient, inconvenient, deficient and in want of improvement."[34]

But how far had things changed by the end of the 19th century when the Corporation policies were more expansive and more ambitious, and education, health and street improvement became the municipal concerns. The Mayor of Worcester had always been protector of the orphans - a duty steadily widening into an obligation to educate absolutely everyone. This was demonstrated in October 1896 with an impressive civic opening of the Victoria Institute, a magnificent pile of brick and terracotta, - a progressive design concept to house a School of Art and Science, a Library and a Museum and Gallery on a single site.

Worthies from the Guildhall by this time, were members of the earliest education committee, the School Board. On appropriate occasions, it therefore became the custom for Worcester's respectful school children to sing the School Board Anthem.

The Worcester School Board Anthem

O God our Chairman bless
And give his work success:
The children's friend.
May he encouraged be,
And may he ever see
His labours crowned by Thee
God bless our friend.

Miss Westcombe likewise bless
Whose loving gentleness
Has won our love.
Thy choicest gifts in store'.
On her be pleased to pour
And may she evermore
Thy goodness prove.

The School Board also bless
O, May their work progress
God bless our school.
May education's power
Help in temptation's hour
The young who are their dower
God bless our school.

(There is also a fourth verse)

The Council had also become increasingly active in health matters since those early days of the cholera, when the Mayor had begged Dr. Charles Hastings, "Save us from this pestilence." The 'clean party' on the Council went vigorously to work and in 1858 constructed a large municipal waterworks at Barbourne, though the filtration equipment essential for preventing typhoid and scarlet fever was not deemed affordable until 1894.

One of the new class of professional officer now seen at the Guildhall was Dr. William Strange, the Medical Officer of Health, a talented and experienced physician capable of attacking Worcester's evil malaise of childhood illness - blamed for two out of five deaths. The Sanitary Inspector of the 1890s, W. Pacey, was also [35]anxious to tackle the problems of the city's overcrowded small dwellings and their heavy reliance on communal privies.

In a host of other ways, the Council now displayed its growing concern with ordinary life - widening the streets to ease traffic flow, erecting urinals and horse drinking troughs all over town, and helping those poor families swamped out in the terrible floods of 1886. Health remained a priority into the new century. In the Great War there was the food rationing organised through the Council's Emergency Committee. Afterwards came the challenge of demolishing Worcester's worst slums, using an old military tank, and moving many of the residents into the new council housing. In those days, strange though it seems, hope for a healthy prosperous age centred on the Corporation owned Electricity Works. In the 1930s anyone wanting to find out more about Worcester was instructed to apply there, not at the Guildhall. Unsurprisingly it also had strong critics like L.T.C. Rolt, author of the well known guide to Worcestershire, who castigated the Electricity Works as an ugly monument to new municipal power politics - "a symbol of the swollen power state."[36]

But it was total war in 1939 which brought the Guildhall closest to the centre of things - the more so because Worcestershire was designated as the possible alternative site of government had London fallen. The Guildhall was never busier. The Mayoress, Mrs Moore Ede, led an indefatigable band of ladies whose motto was "The WRVS never says no" The Guildhall secretaries demonstrated the vital importance of wearing a gas mask, and how you made yourself comfortable in an Anderson shelter.

With the peace in 1945 came a chance to take stock. A dramatic post war reconstruction plan for the city proposed complete transformation as though Worcester had been bombed out like Coventry. Siting the Guildhall in its own square was one inspiring theme of the bold new master plan but other aspects of it were too crude, too brutal to the ancient fabric. In the end, the Council rejected everything - good ideas with the bad. The many copies of the report with their lavish illustrations and copious statistics were dumped unceremoniously in the cellars.[37] The future of Worcester had once again been postponed.

References

1   John Noake: *Worcester in Olden Times.* (Longman)

2   Diarmaid MacCulloch: 'Worcester a Cathedral City in the Reformation' in *The Reformation in English Towns* (Macmillan) Edited by Patrick Collinson and John Craig.

3   Alan Dyer: *Worcester in the Sixteenth Century* (University of Leicester Press)

4   Diarmaid MacCulloch: op cit.

5   Shelagh Bond: *"The Chamber Order Book of Worcester 1602-1650"* (WHS)

6   Quoted in Bill Gwilliams: *Old Worcester : People and Places* (Halfshire Books)

7   Nikolas Pevsner: *The Buildings of England; Worcestershire.* (Penguin Books).

8   David Whitehead: 18c Worcester. article in *The Charter Book of Worcester.* (Revelstone Publishing)

9   Tim Bridges: *A Day Out in Worcester.* (BBC Sound Archive)

10   W. S. Symonds: *Hanley Castle.* (Capella Archive Press, Malvern) This is the myth at its most powerful.

11   Bill Gwilliam: *Old Worcester : People and Places* (Halfshire Books) I am grateful to Bill Gwilliam for this and so much other information.

12   John Noake: *'A Worthy of Worcester's Autobiography'* (Notes - as dictated to his daughter, Laura Mary. (unpublished MSS presented to the author when Mayor of Worcester)

13   C. A. F. Meekings: *'The Chamber of Worcester'* (Transactions of the Worcester Archaeological Society Vol.8 1982)

14   Michael J Franklin: *Sir William Jones.* (University of Wales Press. 1995)

15   Michael J Franklin: *Sir William Jones.* (University of Wales Press. 1995)

16   Michael Grundy: Article in Memory Lane, Evening News.

17   I am grateful to Michael Grundy for noting this quote from a Berrow's Worcester Journal of 1898.

18   David Cannadine: *The Decline and Fall of the British Aristocracy.* (Yale)

19   R. W. Binns: *Worcester Pottery and Porcelain 1752-1851.*

20   See minutes of the Royal Commission on the Worcester Election of 1906.

21   Charles Saxton: *The Origin and Progress of the Worcester Cooperative Society Limited 1881-1931.*

22 Valentine Green: *The History and Antiquities of the City and the Suburbs of Worcester*. 1796.

23 Plan published in the *Building News* of 26 August 1881 where the room is marked as the council chamber.

24 Bentley's *History, Guide and Directory*, Vol. 1, Part 3; Birmingham 1840.

25 Suz Winspear: *Worcester's Lost Theatre*. (Parkburn)

26 John Noake: autobiographical notes. op.cit.

27 T. C. Turberville op. cit. *Worcestershire in the Nineteenth Century*. (Longman 1852) and for other 19c references on this page.

28 T. C. Turberville op. cit. See also the local press accounts of the Guildhall meeting of 23rd February 1842.

29 Letter to *Berrow's Worcester Journal*, 1894.

30 Election address for the 1773 Election.

31 E. P. Thompson: *Beyond the Cold War*. (Merlin Press)

32 John Noake: autobiographical notes. op.cit.

33 David Whitehead: Guide to St. Swithin's. (Churches Conservation Trust) - an exemplary church guide.

34 T. C. Turberville op. cit.

35 D. A. Attwood: I am grateful for the information from this unpublished Mss on *The Growth of Nineteenth Century Worcester*.

36 L.T.C. Rolt: Worcestershire. (Hale).

37 Minoprio & Spencely: *An Outline Development Plan for the County of the City of Worcester. Prepared for the Reconstruction and Development Committee of the City Council*. 1946. also Glaisyer et al. County Town. A Civic Survey for the Planning of Worcester. 1946.